LIVES OF THE SAINTS

Volume II

The Monastic Era

Written by Bart Tesoriero

Illustrations by Michael Adams

TABLE OF CONTENTS

Library of Congress Control Number: 2012905937
ISBN 1-61796-049-9

SAINT APOLLONIA

Feast Day: February 9

Patron of Dentists

Saint Apollonia was born in Egypt. She preached the word of God all her life and risked persecution for her faith. In the year 249, Saint Apollonia was arrested. She told the judge, "I am a Christian and I love and serve the true God." He became very angry and tortured Apollonia. She stood firm and refused to deny Christ even when her persecutors smashed her teeth and knocked them out of her mouth. They threatened to burn her to death unless she denied Jesus. Rather than renounce her faith in Christ, Apollonia threw herself into the raging fire where she perished. When the pagans saw her heroism, many were converted.

Today, Saint Apollonia is recognized as the patron of dentists.

Prayer to Saint Apollonia for Dentists

Dear Saint Apollonia, you comforted many people during your life. By suffering the loss of your teeth and not fearing the fire meant to extinguish your faith, you won the crown of martyrdom and eternal happiness. Please bless all who work in dentistry. Help them to comfort and heal others. Amen.

Saint Apollonia, pray for us.

SAINT SEBASTIAN

Feast Day: January 20

Patron of Athletes

Saint Sebastian was born in Rome in the third century. Because of his noble birth and his bravery, the Emperor Diocletian made Sebastian a captain of his Imperial Guard.

Secretly a Christian, Sebastian healed the sick and led many to the Faith. When the emperor learned this, he ordered his soldiers to shoot Sebastian with arrows. By God's grace and because of his own physical fitness, Sebastian survived. For this reason, he is remembered today as the patron of athletes.

The emperor was very angry when he heard that Sebastian was still alive, and he ordered his soldiers to club him to death. Saint Sebastian died a true soldier for Jesus Christ.

Prayer to Saint Sebastian for Athletes

Glorious Saint Sebastian, although you were shot with arrows and left for dead, you survived because God helped you and you were so strong. You kept your faith in Christ even when the soldiers beat you, because you were so strong in your spirit. Therefore you won the prize of eternal life. Please ask God to bless all athletes. Help them and all of us to love Our Lord Jesus with all our hearts, souls, minds, and strength. Amen.

Saint Sebastian, pray for us!

SAINT BARBARA

Feast Day: December 4

Patroness of Builders and Architects

Saint Barbara was born in the 3rd century. Her pagan father hid her in a lonely tower. While he was away, Barbara had builders install a third window to honor the Holy Trinity.

When her father saw what she had done, he dragged her to the Roman governor. The governor ordered his soldiers to torture Barbara and cut off her head. Barbara held on to her faith in Jesus, and in a rage, her father drew his sword and beheaded her himself. On his way home he was struck and killed by a flash of lightning. Saint Barbara is honored as the patron of architects, because of her imprisonment in the tower.

Prayer to Saint Barbara for Architects

Dear Saint Barbara, your great love for the Holy Trinity moved you to witness to God through architecture. By preparing a place for Christ in your heart, you won a place for yourself in the house of your Heavenly Father.

Dear God, through the prayers of Saint Barbara, please bless all architects and builders who continue Your work of creation. In Jesus' name. Amen.

Saint Barbara, pray for us.

SAINT ADRIAN OF NICOMEDIA

Feast Day: September 8

Patron of Correction Officers

Adrian was a member of the palace guard for the Roman Emperor. One day he was presiding over the torture of Christians. Adrian asked them what reward they expected to receive from God. They replied, quoting from Saint Paul's Epistle to the Corinthians, "Eye has not seen, nor ear heard, neither has it entered into the heart of man, the things which God has prepared for them that love Him."

Moved by the joyful courage of these men, Saint Adrian decided to join them, becoming a believer like his wife. The emperor put Adrian in prison and tortured him. His limbs were crushed by anvils and then cut off along with his head. Adrian was martyred around 304 A.D. Today, Saint Adrian of Nicomedia is the patron of correction officers.

Prayer to Saint Adrian for Correction Officers

Glorious Saint Adrian, by guarding the prisoners in your custody, you discovered the key to your own freedom. Help all who work in corrections to be as vigilant as you were in seeking the truth and as valiant as you upon finding it. Bless and safeguard all correction officers. Amen.

Saint Adrian of Nicomedia, pray for us.

SAINT CATHERINE OF ALEXANDRIA

Feast Day: November 25

Patron of Secretaries

Saint Catherine was a noble Catholic virgin of Alexandria, Egypt. At the age of 18, she told the emperor that he was wrong to persecute Christians. He sent 50 pagan philosophers to argue with her, but Catherine converted them! The emperor ordered Catherine to be imprisoned and scourged. In prison Catherine converted the emperor's wife and 200 of his soldiers. The emperor became very angry when he heard this. He ordered Catherine to be executed on a spiked wheel. It shattered at her touch, and he beheaded Catherine in 305 AD.

Devotion to Saint Catherine spread during the Crusades. Students, teachers, and others asked for her patronage.

Prayer to Saint Catherine for Secretaries

Glorious Saint Catherine, virgin and martyr, you spoke tirelessly of God to all who would listen, neither breaking nor turning away from Him even though tortured. Inspire, by your holy example, all who work serving others as secretaries. May their commitment to Jesus, who is the Way, the Truth, and the Life, be total and true. Amen.

Saint Catherine of Alexandria, pray for us!

SAINT BLAISE

Feast Day: February 3

Patron of Veterinarians

According to legend, Blaise was born into a wealthy Christian family and trained as a doctor. He was ordained a bishop at a young age and he escaped the persecution of Diocletian by retiring to the hills and living as a hermit. In the wilderness, wild animals would come to him for healing and gather around his cave. Blaise would walk among them unafraid. One day the huntsmen of the Roman governor saw the wild animals gathered outside his cave and investigated. Discovering the bishop, they brought him before the governor, who tortured Blaise, but to no avail. Steadfast to the end, Blaise was finally beheaded around the year 316. Because he cared so well for animals, Saint Blaise is remembered today as the patron of veterinarians.

Prayer to Saint Blaise for Veterinarians

Dear Saint Blaise, please bless all veterinarians who work with animals. Help them to know the best ways of treating all the animals they see every day and comforting their owners. Help them to be as tender as you were with the wild animals and as firm as you were in the defense of the Faith. Amen.

Saint Blaise, pray for us. 15

SAINT NICHOLAS

Feast Day: December 6

Patron of Children and Sailors

Saint Nicholas was born in a province of Asia Minor during the third century. His parents were devout Christians and extremely wealthy. They died while Nicholas was still young. He gave all his money to help the poor, the sick, and children in need. He often helped others in secret. Nicholas was sent to live in a monastery and became one of the youngest priests ever.

Nicholas dedicated his life to serving God and others. In the early part of the fourth century he was made Bishop of Myra. It was said that he was not just able to nurse sick children back to health—he could raise them from the dead! Saint Nicholas died in 342 A.D. and is recognized as the protector and patron of all children and of sailors.

Prayer to Saint Nicholas for Children and Sailors

Dear Saint Nicholas, please bless all children and help them to know and love Jesus. You once appeared to sailors during a great storm and helped them to float safely into port. Please bless all sailors with grace and peace. Amen.

Saint Nicholas, pray for us.

SAINT AUGUSTINE

Feast Day: August 28

Patron of Theologians and Printers

Saint Augustine was born in 354, in Africa. He was smart and popular. However, his heart was far from God. His mother, Monica, prayed every day that God would help her son. After 33 years, God answered Saint Monica's prayers. Augustine asked Jesus to come into his heart, and God gave Augustine the gift of faith. He was baptized and gave all his goods to the poor. He became a bishop and fought the enemies of the Church by his life, preaching, and writing. "Our hearts are made for You, O Lord," he wrote, "and they are restless until they rest in You." Saint Augustine died in 430.

Prayer to Saint Augustine for Theologians and Printers

Dear Saint Augustine, you loved Jesus very much. You studied to know Jesus better, so that you could love Him more. Please bless all men and women who study about God. Through your prayers, may God help them to know Him better, to love Him more, and to serve Him with joy.

Please bless all who print books so others can learn about God and the amazing world He has created. Amen.

Saint Augustine, pray for us.

SAINT PATRICK

Feast Day: March 17

Patron of Ireland and of Engineers

Saint Patrick was born around 389. At the age of 16, he was captured by pirates who took him to Ireland. Patrick stayed close to Jesus and the Catholic Faith. Six years later he escaped, and after many trials made his way home.

Patrick saw in a dream all the children of Ireland stretching out their hands from the wombs of their mothers, and crying to him. God showed Patrick that he was to return to Ireland and tell the people about Jesus.

Patrick returned to Ireland where he was made Bishop, and he traveled all over Ireland bringing the Faith. He restored sight to the blind, health to the sick, and raised the dead to life. He died on March 17 in the year 461.

Prayer to Saint Patrick for Ireland and Engineers

Dear Saint Patrick, you preached the good news of Jesus to the people of Ireland. You built many churches and monasteries. Please bless all engineers and help them to build good things for others. Help all of us to love one another and to trust Christ as you did. Amen!

Saint Patrick, pray for us!

SAINT BENEDICT

Feast Day: July 11

Patron of Monks and Explorers

Saint Benedict was born in 480, to a noble Roman family. Because of the wickedness of the people, he left Rome and journeyed to a cave deep in a mountain. He lived alone there for three years. God gave Saint Benedict the power to work miracles. He spoke God's Word and saw visions of heaven. He served the poor and taught people about the Gospel. In time, other men came to stay with him. They formed the Benedictine Order of monks.

Saint Benedict and his monks moved to Monte Cassino. They built an Abbey, and there Saint Benedict wrote his rule for monastic life. His rule is simply: *Pray and Work.* Saint Benedict died at Monte Cassino with his hands lifted in prayer to the heavens, in the year 547.

Prayer to Saint Benedict for Monks and Explorers

Dear Saint Benedict, many men wanted to be around you because you were both holy and kind. Help all monks to be true to the Lord and to grow in love for all people. Bless also all those who explore new lands and new ways to help people become all that God wants them to be. Amen.

Saint Benedict, pray for us.

SAINT ISIDORE OF SEVILLE

Feast Day: April 4

Patron of the Internet and Computer Technicians

Isidore was born of a royal family in Spain in 560. He didn't get very good grades, so he ran away from school. He stopped for a drink of water from a spring, and noticed a stone, which was hollowed out by the dripping water. He realized that if he kept working at it, little by little, just like that dripping water, he could do great things. He returned to school, and by hard work he became a great bishop and teacher of the Faith.

Saint Isidore wrote 20 books which make up the first Christian Encyclopedia. Because of his ability to help people understand facts, Saint Isidore is the patron saint of the Internet and of computer technicians and programmers. Saint Isidore died on April 4, 636.

Prayer to Saint Isidore for Computer Technicians

O Saint Isidore, your love for God led you to study the Book of Nature and to preserve the wisdom of the whole world. Inspire those who work as computer technicians to use their skills to help us grow in true wisdom and service. Amen.

Saint Isidore, pray for us!

SAINT DYMPHNA

Feast Day: May 15

Patron of Counselors, Psychologists

Saint Dymphna was born in Ireland to a pagan chief named Damon and a Christian mother. When Dymphna was 14, her beloved mother died. Her father became mentally ill with sadness. His evil counselors told him to take his daughter as a wife. Saint Dymphna fled to Belgium, but her father found her and told her to return to Ireland as his bride. When she refused, he drew his sword and struck off her head. Saint Dymphna was martyred around 620 A.D. Many sick people have been healed at her shrine, built on the spot where she was buried. Saint Dymphna is the patron of counselors.

Prayer to Saint Dymphna for Counselors

Dear Saint Dymphna, through your prayers many people have been healed of mental illness. Please help and bless all counselors. Help them to bring healing, comfort, and compassion to the confused and the sick in their care.

Lord God, through the prayers of Saint Dymphna, pour out Your Spirit of wisdom and good counsel on all who advise others, that they may always glorify You and lead all Your children to You. In Jesus' name. Amen.

Saint Dymphna, pray for us!

27

SAINT ISIDORE THE FARMER

Feast Day: May 15

Patron of Farmers and Farm Workers

Isidore was born in Madrid, Spain, around the year 1070. He rose up early every morning to go to Mass. Then he would go to work in the fields. One day some farm workers complained that Isidore was always late for work. When the master investigated, he found that an angel plowed the field while Isidore prayed.

Isidore married Maria Torribia, who is also a canonized saint. The couple had one son, but he died in his youth. Isidore died on May 15, 1130. Many miracles and cures are reported at his grave. Today, Saint Isidore is venerated as the patron of farmers.

Prayer to Saint Isidore for Farmers

Dear Saint Isidore, you let the seed of the Gospel take root in you and produce good fruit. Please pray that we will allow Jesus to live in us as you did. Dear God, through the prayers of Saint Isidore, please bless all farmers and farm laborers to love You and serve others. Please keep them safe and protect them. Supply their needs, as they supply food for us. In Jesus' name. Amen.

Saint Isidore the Farmer, pray for us.

SAINT FRANCIS OF ASSISI

Feast Day: October 4

Patron of Animals and All Who Care for the Earth

Saint Francis was born as the son of a wealthy merchant in Assisi in 1182. He loved to sing songs and have fun with his friends. One day, Jesus spoke to Francis from the crucifix in the tiny chapel of San Damiano. He said, "Go, rebuild My Church." Francis fell in love with Jesus. He gave away his rich clothing and wore poor clothes. He cared for the sick and needy. He taught that everything God made, like the sun, the moon, the animals and plants, is good. God wants us to take good care of our earth. Francis gathered many followers and set about spiritually rebuilding the Church.

The pope blessed Saint Francis and his followers. Saint Francis prayed and preached much. He received the wounds of Jesus, and died with the words, "Welcome, Sister Death!"

Prayer to Saint Francis for the Care of our Earth

Dear Saint Francis, you loved Jesus with all your heart. You allowed Him to live His life through you. Please bless all who care for others as you did. Bless those who care for the earth and all God's creatures. Help us to love one another. Amen.

Saint Francis of Assisi, pray for us.

THE MONASTIC ERA

As the Church grew and the culture changed, God continued to choose heroes and heroines of Faith to help new generations of believers follow Him. One of these was Saint Benedict, who left the hustle and bustle of Rome to seek God in the quiet of a cave. He founded Monte Cassino, the first great monastery of the West. He also wrote a Rule of life for all monks and nuns. The Rule of Saint Benedict has deeply affected not only those who lived it, but all of Western Civilization, to this very day.

Women saints of this era, like Saint Dymphna, became patrons for groups of people. Her shrine in Gheel, Belgium, has been a place of hope for thousands of pilgrims seeking emotional healing since the 13th century.

Saint Francis of Assisi, who lived about 700 years after Saint Benedict, was a new kind of monk. Before, monks and nuns were supported by their work on the lands they owned. Saint Francis and his followers begged for their food, so as to live more fully like Jesus, who was poor so we could become rich.

Dear Saints of the Monastic Era, thank you for devoting yourselves to prayer and work, so as to build up the Church and the world. Help us also to seek first the kingdom of heaven, and then to serve our neighbors. Amen.